SCRATCH CODE CHALLENGE

Scratch Code
SMART HOMES

Max
Wainewright

CRABTREE
PUBLISHING COMPANY
WWW.CRABTREEBOOKS.COM

CRABTREE
PUBLISHING COMPANY
WWW.CRABTREEBOOKS.COM

Author: Max Wainewright

Editorial director: Kathy Middleton

Editors: Elise Short, Crystal Sikkens

Proofreader: Melissa Boyce

Design: Matt Lilly

Cover design: Peter Scoulding

Illustrations: John Haslam

Prepress technician: Margaret Amy Salter

Print coordinator: Katherine Berti

Every attempt has been made to clear copyright. Should there be any inadvertent omission please apply to the publisher for rectification.

Picture credits:
Shutterstock: NicoElNino 6, VCoscaron 12, petrmalinak 14, Andrey_Popov 18, Sean Pavone 24, Photographicss 28, Dreamstime: GarcÃa Juan 26.

We recommend that children are supervised at all times when using the Internet. Some of the projects in this series use a computer webcam or microphone. Please make sure children are made aware that they should only allow a computer to access the webcam or microphone on specific websites that a trusted adult has told them to use. We do not recommend children use websites or microphones on any other websites other than those mentioned in this book.

The website addresses (URLs) included in this book were valid at the time of going to press. However, it is possible that contents or addresses may have changed since the publication of this book. No responsibility for any such changes can be accepted by either the author or the Publisher.

Scratch is developed by the Lifelong Kindergarten Group at the MIT Media Lab. See http://scratch.mit.edu.

Images and illustrations from Scratch included in this book have been developed by the Lifelong Kindergarten Group at the MIT Media Lab (see http://scratch.mit.edu) and made available under the Creative Commons Attribution-ShareAlike 2.0 license (https://creativecommons.org/licenses/by-sa/2.0/deed.en). The third party trademarks used in this book are the property of their respective owners, including the Scratch name and logo. The owners of these trademarks have not endorsed, authorized, or sponsored this book.

Library and Archives Canada Cataloguing in Publication

Title: Scratch code smart homes / Max Wainewright.
Other titles: Smart homes
Names: Wainewright, Max, author.
Description: Series statement: Scratch code challenge |
  Includes index.
Identifiers: Canadiana (print) 20190106948 |
  Canadiana (ebook) 20190106956 |
  ISBN 9780778765400 (hardcover) |
  ISBN 9780778765684 (softcover) |
  ISBN 9781427123855 (HTML)
Subjects: LCSH: Home automation—Juvenile literature. | LCSH:
  Dwellings—Computer programs—Juvenile literature. | LCSH:
  Scratch (Computer program language)—Juvenile literature. |
  LCSH: Computer programming—Juvenile literature.
Classification: LCC TK7881.25 .W35 2019 | j643/.6—dc23

Library of Congress Cataloging-in-Publication Data

Names: Wainewright, Max, author.
Title: Scratch code smart homes / Max Wainewright.
Other titles: Smart homes
Description: New York, New York : Crabtree Publishing, 2020.
  | Series: Scratch code challenge | "First published in Great
  Britain in 2019 by Wayland." | Includes index.
Identifiers: LCCN 2019013623 (print) | LCCN 2019014504 (ebook)
  ISBN 9781427123855 (Electronic) |
  ISBN 9780778765400 (hardcover : alk. paper) |
  ISBN 9780778765684 (pbk. : alk. paper)
Subjects: LCSH: Home automation--Juvenile literature. |
  Dwellings--Computer programs--Juvenile literature. |
  Scratch (Computer program language)--Juvenile literature. |
  Computer programming--Juvenile literature.
Classification: LCC TK7881.25 (ebook) |
  LCC TK7881.25 .W35 2020 (print) | DDC 643/.6--dc23
LC record available at https://lccn.loc.gov/2019013623

Crabtree Publishing Company

www.crabtreebooks.com   1–800–387–7650

Published by Crabtree Publishing Company in 2020

Text copyright © ICT Apps, 2019
Art and design copyright © Hodder and Stoughton, 2019

Printed in the U.S.A./072019/CG20190501

Published in Canada
Crabtree Publishing
616 Welland Ave.
St. Catharines, Ontario
L2M 5V6

Published in the United States
Crabtree Publishing
PMB 59051
350 Fifth Avenue, 59th Floor
New York, New York 10118

Contents

Introduction 4

Project: Smart Homes 6

Project: Intercom and Camera 12

Project: Voice Control 1 and 2 14

Project: Home Robots 18

Project: Burglar Alarm 24

Bugs and Debugging 30

Glossary 31

Index and Further Information 32

Words in *italics* appear in the glossary on page 31.

Introduction

In this book, you will learn how computer technology is used in modern homes and buildings. You'll find out about how this technology is changing the way we live, making our lives easier and our homes more secure.

We'll spend some time looking at how some devices use smart technology. We will also have a look inside the computer code that connects the components and brings devices to life.

You'll use the *algorithms* and ideas that are used to control devices within buildings to create your own coding programs. These programs will help you understand how things work, and set you on the road to dreaming up your own ideas for a house of the future!

There are a lot of different ways to create code. We will be using a website called Scratch to do our coding.

Type **scratch.mit.edu** into your web browser, then click Create to start a new project.

Let's start by looking at the important parts of the screen in Scratch:

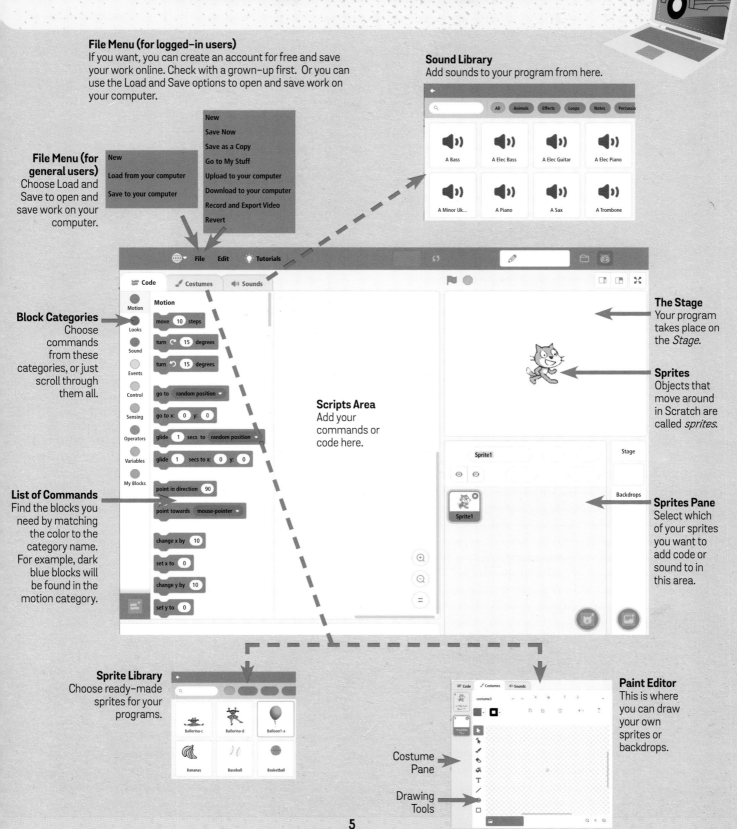

File Menu (for logged-in users)
If you want, you can create an account for free and save your work online. Check with a grown-up first. Or you can use the Load and Save options to open and save work on your computer.

Sound Library
Add sounds to your program from here.

File Menu (for general users)
Choose Load and Save to open and save work on your computer.

New
Load from your computer
Save to your computer

New
Save Now
Save as a Copy
Go to My Stuff
Upload to your computer
Download to your computer
Record and Export Video
Revert

All Animals Effects Loops Notes Percussion

A Bass   A Elec Bass   A Elec Guitar   A Elec Piano
A Minor Uk...   A Piano   A Sax   A Trombone

Block Categories
Choose commands from these categories, or just scroll through them all.

List of Commands
Find the blocks you need by matching the color to the category name. For example, dark blue blocks will be found in the motion category.

Code   Costumes   Sounds

Motion
Looks
Sound
Events
Control
Sensing
Operators
Variables
My Blocks

Motion

move 10 steps
turn 15 degrees
turn 15 degrees
go to random position
go to x: 0 y: 0
glide 1 secs to random position
glide 1 secs to x: 0 y: 0
point in direction 90
point towards mouse-pointer
change x by 10
set x to 0
change y by 10
set y to 0

Scripts Area
Add your commands or code here.

The Stage
Your program takes place on the *Stage*.

Sprites
Objects that move around in Scratch are called *sprites*.

Sprite1   Stage
Sprite1   Backdrops

Sprites Pane
Select which of your sprites you want to add code or sound to in this area.

Sprite Library
Choose ready-made sprites for your programs.

Ballerina-c   Ballerina-d   Balloon1-a
Bananas   Baseball   Basketball

Code   Costumes   Sounds
costume3

Paint Editor
This is where you can draw your own sprites or backdrops.

Costume Pane

Drawing Tools

5

Smart Homes

Technology has always played a big role in homes and other buildings. Over 2,000 years ago, the ancient Romans invented a *system* that used hot air under floors to heat homes. Homes used to be lit with candles. This gave way to gas-powered and then electric lights. Today, new inventions continue to improve buildings.

Computers are now taking an ever-increasing role in how different parts of a building work. Let's build our own house with code to see how this works. The house will have a number of automatic lights and music that switch on and off as the Scratch Cat walks around.

STEP 1 – **The Stage**

We need to draw the background first, so click **Stage** in the **Sprites pane**.

Stage

Backdrops

STEP 2 – **The Backdrop**

🖌 Backdrops

Click the **Backdrops** tab.

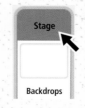

For help, go to:
www.maxw.com

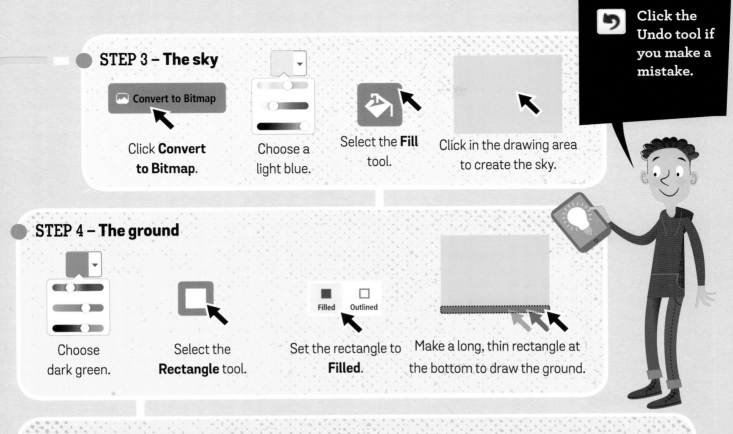

STEP 3 – The sky

Click Convert to Bitmap.

Choose a light blue.

Select the **Fill** tool.

Click in the drawing area to create the sky.

Click the Undo tool if you make a mistake.

STEP 4 – The ground

Choose dark green.

Select the **Rectangle** tool.

Filled   Outlined

Set the rectangle to **Filled**.

Make a long, thin rectangle at the bottom to draw the ground.

STEP 5 – Draw the house

We need to draw things inside the house, so just draw a simple silhouette of the house in white.

Choose white.

Use the mouse to draw a large rectangle for the main part of the house.

Pick the **Line** tool.

Make the line thicker.

Draw three lines to give the house a roof.

Choose the **Fill** tool.

Click inside the roof to fill it in with white. (If the color leaks outside the house, click **Undo** and look for any gaps between your lines. Join them up.)

STEP 6 – Get coding

We need the cat to be outside the house when the program starts.

Click on the cat in the **Sprites pane** to make sure you assign the code to the cat, not the house.

Sprite 1

Click the **Code** tab.

Now drag in this code:

when 🏳 **clicked** ← Run this code when the green flag is clicked:

go to x: -210 y: -115 ← Set the x and y coordinates to move the cat to the left of the screen (see page 30).

go to front ▾ layer ← Bring it in front of any other sprites.

set size to 50% ← Shrink the cat down to half its normal size.

🏳 **Click the green flag to test this part of the code.**

STEP 7 – Move it

Now drag these four separate sections of code into the **Scripts Area** to make the cat move.

when up arrow ▾ key pressed ← Run this code when the up arrow key is pressed:

change y by 10 ← Change the y coordinate of the cat by 10.

when left arrow ▾ key pressed ← Run this code when the left arrow key is pressed:

change x by -10 ← Change the x coordinate of the cat by –10.

when right arrow ▾ key pressed ← Run this code when the right arrow key is pressed:

change x by 10 ← Change the x coordinate by 10.

when down arrow ▾ key pressed ← Run this code when the down arrow key is pressed:

change y by -10 ← Change the y coordinate of the cat by –10.

🏳 **Click the green flag. Check that the cat moves in the correct direction when each arrow key is pressed.**

STEP 8 – Make a room

Let's draw the first room. To keep things simple, just draw a rectangle. In order to switch the light off and on depending on whether the cat is in the room, we need the rectangle to be a sprite.

Hover over the **Choose a Sprite** button.

Click the **Brush** *icon*.

Click **Convert to Bitmap**.

Select the **Rectangle** tool.

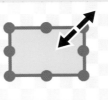

Drag out a yellow rectangle. (Yellow will stand for the room being lit.)

In the storage area, drag your new room sprite inside the house.

If the room is too big or too small, click the **Arrow** tool in the drawing area.

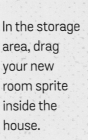

Then click on a corner and drag to adjust the size of the sprite. It should be almost a quarter of the size of the house.

> We need to make the light in each room switch on when the cat walks into it. But before we code our house, let's take a moment to find out how a real smart house uses *sensors* to do this.

How it works

There are many different types of sensors that can be used to detect motion. We'll start by looking at a passive infrared motion detector, or PIR.

If a human being or animal passes through the area of detection, the PIR notices a slight change in temperature. It detects this change because a tiny amount of infrared radiation is emitted by the passerby. The Fresnel lens focuses the radiation onto the PIR.

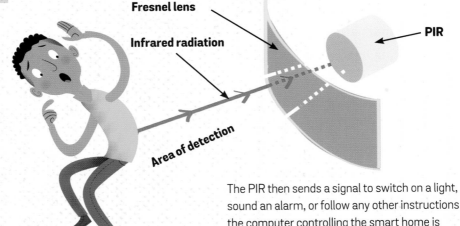

Fresnel lens

Infrared radiation

PIR

Area of detection

The PIR then sends a signal to switch on a light, sound an alarm, or follow any other instructions the computer controlling the smart home is programmed to do.

STEP 9 – Sensor code

☰ Code ✎

Click the **Code** tab. Drag this code into the **Scripts Area** so the room sprite can detect when the cat enters the room.

```
when 🚩 clicked          ◄——— Run this code when the green flag is clicked:
set ghost ▾ effect to 90  ◄——— Make the room sprite transparent and faded out.
forever                   ◄——— Keep looping through this code:
  if ◇ touching Sprite1 ▾ ? then  ◄——— If the room sprite is touching Sprite1 (the cat), then run this code:
    set ghost ▾ effect to 0   ◄——— Turn off the transparent effect—this makes it look like a light has been turned on.
  else                    ◄——— Else: if they are not touching:
    set ghost ▾ effect to 90  ◄——— Make the room sprite transparent again.
  ↰
```

🚩 **Click the green flag to test your code. Use the arrow keys to move the cat into the room, and the light should switch on.**

STEP 10 – More rooms

We can create more rooms by duplicating the first one. This will copy all of the code too.

Spri | **duplicate**
     | delete
     | export

In the **Sprites pane**, *right-click* the room, then click **duplicate**.

Drag the new room into a space in the house.

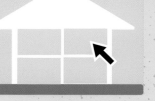

Duplicate two more rooms, and position them like this in your house.

🚩 **Click the green flag to test your code. Use the arrow keys to move the cat around the house. Each light should switch on and off automatically!**

> How about making music play automatically when the cat goes into a room? That would be cool!

STEP 11 – Automatic music

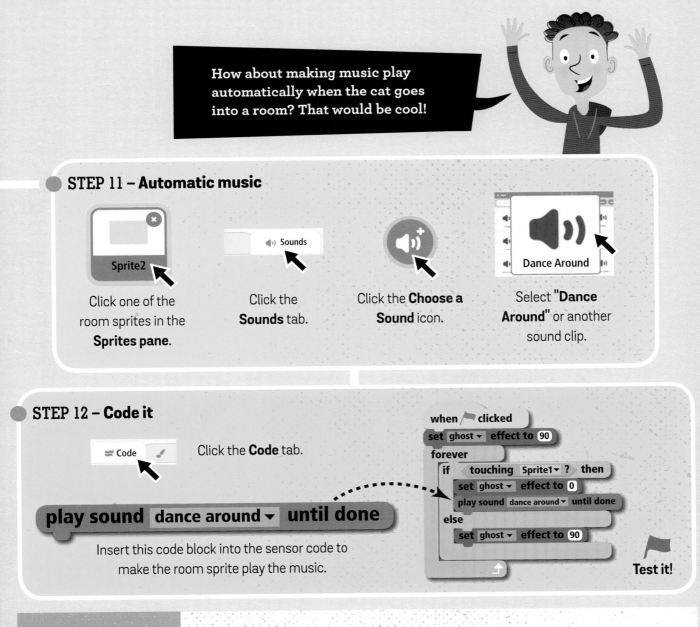

Sprite2

Click one of the room sprites in the **Sprites pane**.

Sounds

Click the **Sounds** tab.

Click the **Choose a Sound** icon.

Dance Around

Select **"Dance Around"** or another sound clip.

STEP 12 – Code it

Code

Click the **Code** tab.

play sound dance around ▾ **until done**

Insert this code block into the sensor code to make the room sprite play the music.

```
when 🏳 clicked
set ghost ▾ effect to 90
forever
    if  touching Sprite1 ▾ ?  then
        set ghost ▾ effect to 0
        play sound dance around ▾ until done
    else
        set ghost ▾ effect to 90
```

Test it!

Investigate

What happens if you try different numbers in the "set ghost effect" *code block*?

Try changing "ghost" to a different effect. How does this change the room sprite?

Code challenge

Try adding more rooms. Could you put one in the attic space at the top?

Add some furniture to the room sprites.

Listen to the other sound effects available. Can you find one that would be good in the bathroom? Maybe you can find one that sounds like water running when the cat enters the room?

Imagine it's a really hot day. How about having a fan that comes on automatically when you walk near it? You'll need to draw a new sprite to be the fan. Make sure you draw it in the middle of the drawing area. Your code will be similar to the room sprites' code, but instead of changing the ghost effect you will need to make the fan rotate when the cat is near it.

Intercom and Camera

The first doorbells were invented nearly 200 years ago. The technology has developed considerably since then, and intercoms with cameras are standard outside apartment buildings and some homes. With mobile technology, it's now possible to see who's knocking at your door even if you are on vacation. As *artificial intelligence (AI)* improves, your house may soon let you in automatically if it recognizes your face.

Now let's create your own doorbell.

STEP 1 – Remove the cat

Right-click on the cat sprite and click **delete**.

STEP 2 – Add a sprite

Click the **Choose a Sprite** icon.

STEP 3 – The button

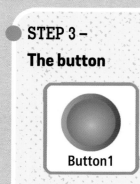

Button1

Scroll through to find **Button1**. Click on it.

STEP 4 – Add the Music Extension

You need to add some extra code blocks to control the sound of the doorbell. This group of code blocks is called an extension.

Click the **Add Extension** button.

Click **Music**.

Music

STEP 5 – Get coding

Drag this code into the **Scripts Area**:

```
when this sprite clicked
♫ set instrument to (16) Vibraphone ▾
♫ play note 63 for 0.5 beats
♫ play note 59 for 1 beats
```

Run this code when the button sprite is clicked:

Choose (16) Vibraphone.

Play note 63 for half a beat.

Play note 59 for one beat.

⚑ Click the green flag to test this part of the code.

If your computer has a webcam, we can add a camera to the doorbell to see who is calling! Remember to only use your webcam with websites you trust and people you know!

STEP 6 – Add the Video Extension

Add some extra code blocks to use the webcam.

Click **Add Extension**.

Video Sensing

Click **Video Sensing**.

STEP 7 – The camera

Modify your code to include the video camera:

```
when this sprite clicked
turn video on ▾
♫ set instrument to (16) Vibraphone ▾
♫ play note 63 for 0.5 beats
♫ play note 59 for 1 beats
wait 5 seconds
turn video off ▾
```

Turn the camera on when the button sprite is clicked.

Wait a moment.

Turn the camera off.

Add this second piece of code to make sure the camera is off when the program starts up.

```
when ⚑ clicked
turn video off ▾
```

✓ **Allow**

If you want your computer to use the camera, then you need to click the **Allow** button the first time the program runs.

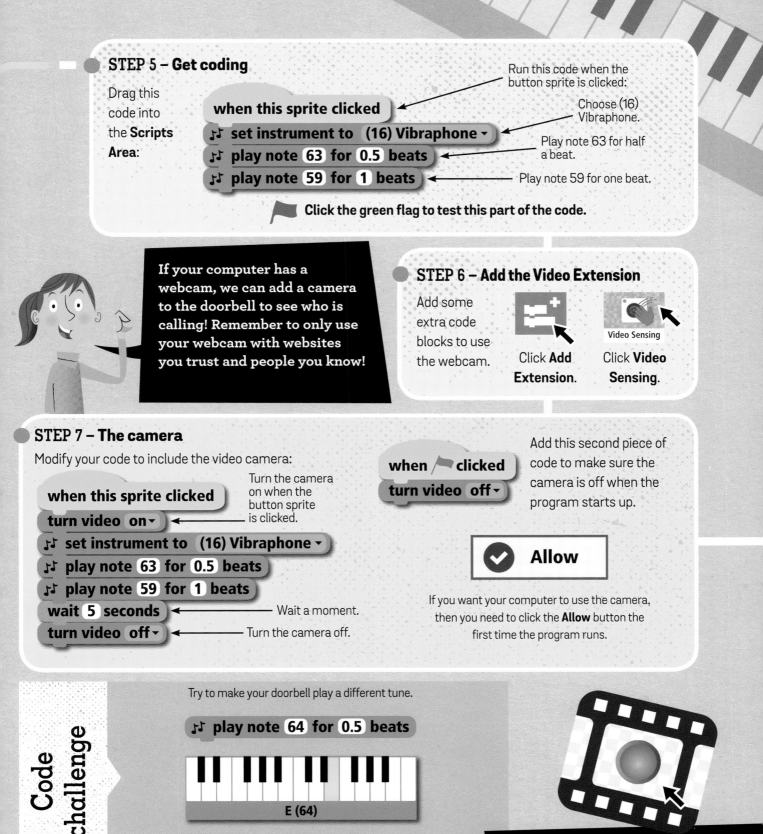

Code challenge

Try to make your doorbell play a different tune.

```
♫ play note 64 for 0.5 beats
```

E (64)

Can you add a second tune? Either add another button with this tune, or work out a way of switching between them.

For help, go to: **www.maxw.com**

13

Voice Control 1

Some modern buildings use voice control technology. Instead of pressing a button to switch on a light or turn up the heat, all you need to do is say "turn lights on." Let's look at how this works, and then try building your own simple version using code.

You need a microphone for your computer to be able to do this project. There may be one built into it.

First, let's take a "look" at the sounds around us by creating a program that can draw a simple *wave form* of the sounds detected by the computer.

Make sure it is selected and turned up by checking the settings menu on your computer.

STEP 1 – **How loud?**

We need a *variable* that can store how loud different sounds are.

Operators

Variables

Click the **Code** tab.

Click the **Variables** category.

Make a Variable

Click **Make a Variable.**

Type **level.**

New variable

New variable name:

level

For all sprites   For this sprite only

More Options

Cancel   OK

Click **OK.**

To let Scratch use your microphone, you need to click the "Allow" button the first time the program runs.

✓ **Allow**

Beware of other websites asking to use your microphone. Check with an adult first.

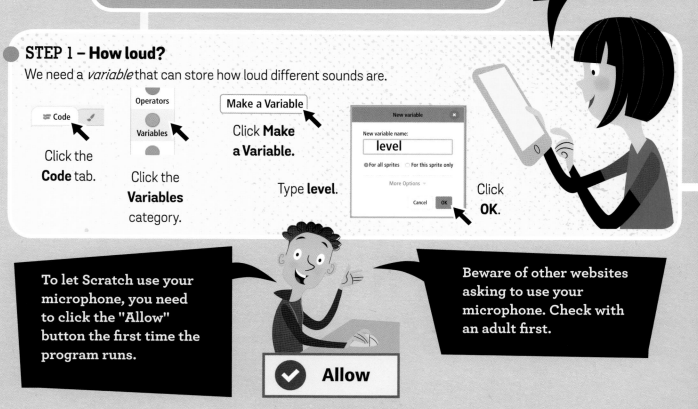

STEP 2 – Add the Pen Extension

Add some extra code blocks to use the pen and drawing blocks.

 Click the **Add Extension** button.

 Click **Pen**.

STEP 3 – The code

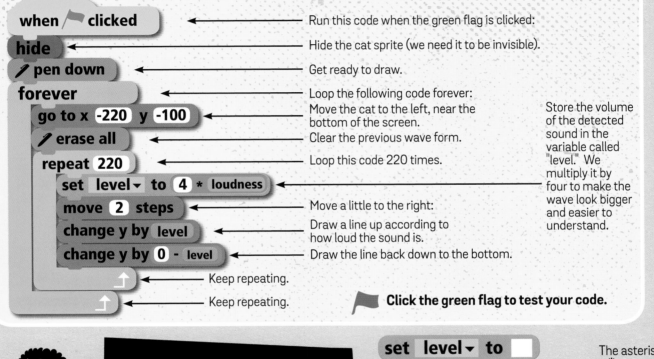

when 🏳 clicked — Run this code when the green flag is clicked:

hide — Hide the cat sprite (we need it to be invisible).

pen down — Get ready to draw.

forever — Loop the following code forever:

go to x -220 y -100 — Move the cat to the left, near the bottom of the screen.

erase all — Clear the previous wave form.

repeat 220 — Loop this code 220 times.

set level to 4 * loudness — Store the volume of the detected sound in the variable called "level." We multiply it by four to make the wave look bigger and easier to understand.

move 2 steps — Move a little to the right:

change y by level — Draw a line up according to how loud the sound is.

change y by 0 - level — Draw the line back down to the bottom.

Keep repeating.

Keep repeating.

🏳 **Click the green flag to test your code.**

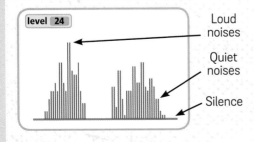

Use calculations in your code by dragging operator blocks within other blocks. Make sure they snap into place correctly.

set level to ☐

set level to ☐ * ☐

set level to 4 * ☐

set level to 4 * loudness

The asterisk * means multiply when we are coding.

How it works

level 24

Loud noises

Quiet noises

Silence

When you run your code, a blue line will start moving across the screen. Speak into your computer's microphone and you should see a wave form appear. Try speaking at different levels, whispering and shouting! The louder your voice, the taller the wave form will be. Try saying different words such as "turn on" and "turn off" to see the "shape" of the sound levels.

If no blue lines appear, or they are very small, check your microphone's settings.

Voice Control 2

Now that we know how to detect the sound levels sensed by the computer, let's make a simple program that turns the lights on or off. The lights will change when our program "hears" a command.

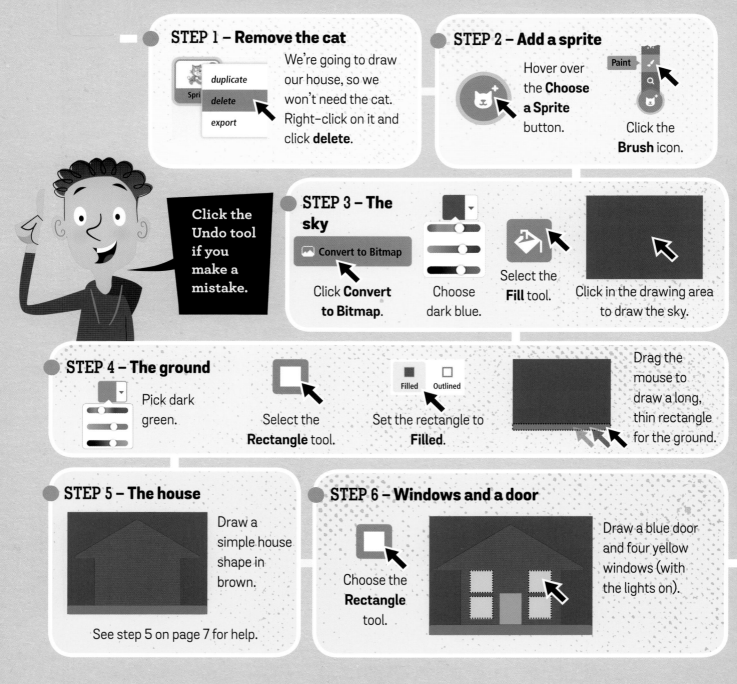

STEP 1 – Remove the cat

We're going to draw our house, so we won't need the cat. Right-click on it and click **delete**.

duplicate
delete
export

STEP 2 – Add a sprite

Hover over the **Choose a Sprite** button.

Paint

Click the **Brush** icon.

Click the Undo tool if you make a mistake.

STEP 3 – The sky

Click **Convert to Bitmap**.

Convert to Bitmap

Choose dark blue.

Select the **Fill** tool.

Click in the drawing area to draw the sky.

STEP 4 – The ground

Pick dark green.

Select the **Rectangle** tool.

Filled   Outlined

Set the rectangle to **Filled**.

Drag the mouse to draw a long, thin rectangle for the ground.

STEP 5 – The house

Draw a simple house shape in brown.

See step 5 on page 7 for help.

STEP 6 – Windows and a door

Choose the **Rectangle** tool.

Draw a blue door and four yellow windows (with the lights on).

STEP 7 – Duplicate costume

We need a second picture of the house with the lights out. Scratch calls this a second "costume." To make this, we will duplicate the first one, then change it.

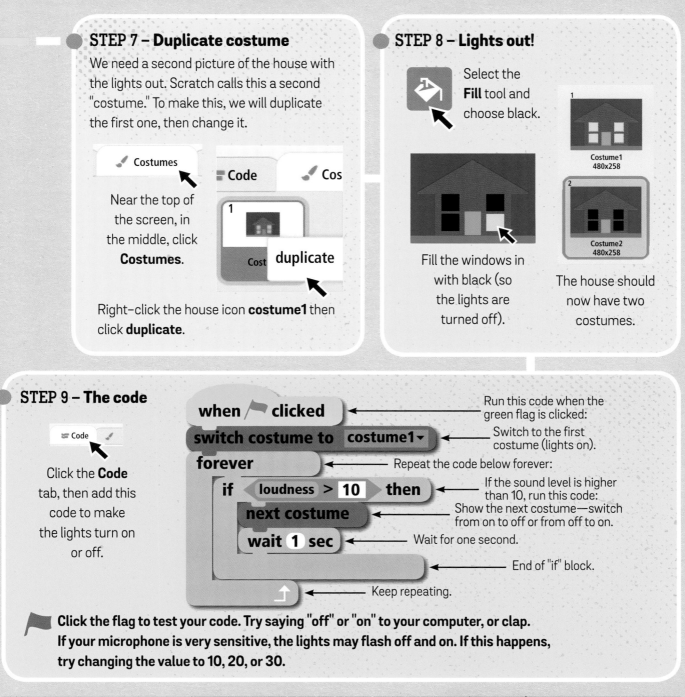

Near the top of the screen, in the middle, click **Costumes**.

Right-click the house icon **costume1** then click **duplicate**.

STEP 8 – Lights out!

Select the **Fill** tool and choose black.

Fill the windows in with black (so the lights are turned off).

Costume1
480x258

Costume2
480x258

The house should now have two costumes.

STEP 9 – The code

Click the **Code** tab, then add this code to make the lights turn on or off.

```
when [flag] clicked
switch costume to costume1
forever
    if  loudness > 10  then
        next costume
        wait 1 sec
```

Run this code when the green flag is clicked:

Switch to the first costume (lights on).

Repeat the code below forever:

If the sound level is higher than 10, run this code:

Show the next costume—switch from on to off or from off to on.

Wait for one second.

End of "if" block.

Keep repeating.

Click the flag to test your code. Try saying "off" or "on" to your computer, or clap. If your microphone is very sensitive, the lights may flash off and on. If this happens, try changing the value to 10, 20, or 30.

How it works

Our program doesn't really know what has been said. It just listens for a sound and then turns the lights on or off. Creating a more sophisticated program that really understands commands is a lot more complex.

To do that, we would need to analyze the shape of the wave form the computer records and compare it to a wave form that says "on" or "off" or other words.

Home Robots

Do you already have a robot in your home? Over the next few years, you may find more robots making their way into your house. They will be cleaning your floors and windows, delivering your shopping, or even painting your walls!

But can robots really perform these kinds of tasks well? Let's have a look at how the code inside them works by making a robot vacuum cleaner.

STEP 1 – Remove the cat

Right-click on the cat sprite and click **delete**.

Our screen robot won't be able to vacuum up real dirt, but it will show us how a robot vacuum cleaner knows how to move around.

STEP 2 – Add a sprite

Hover over the **Choose a Sprite** button.

Click the **Brush** icon.

18

> Now draw your robot vacuum. Make sure you show it in plan view—or drawn from above. It must face to the right.

STEP 3 – Shapes and color

Convert to Bitmap

Click **Convert to Bitmap**.

Choose a silver color for your robot.

Select the **Circle** tool.

Filled Outlined

Choose the **Filled** option.

STEP 4 – Draw the robot

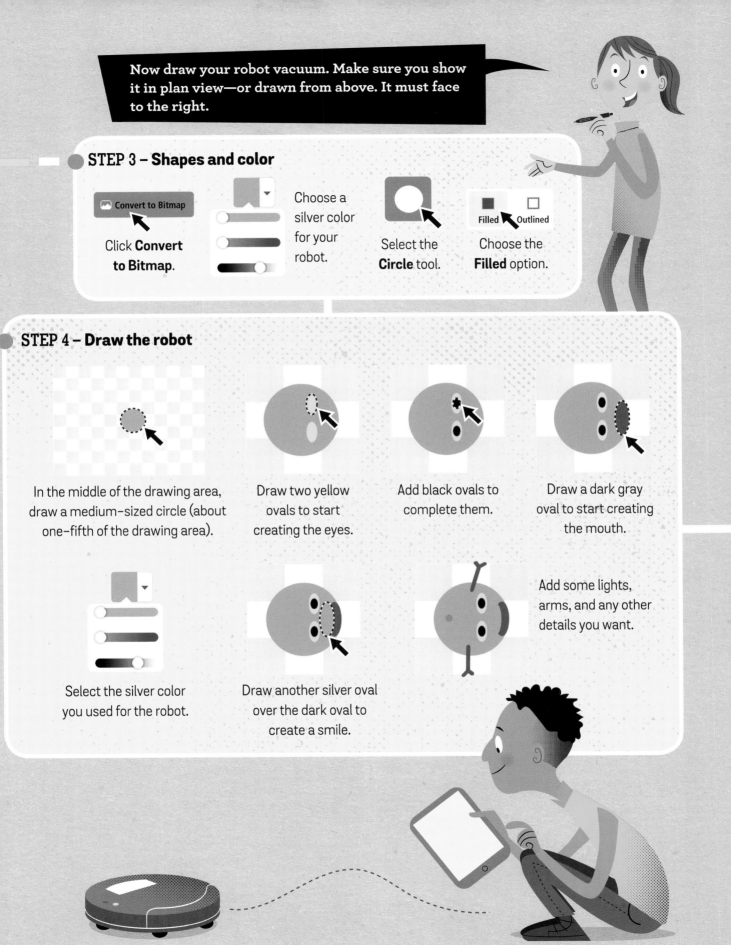

In the middle of the drawing area, draw a medium-sized circle (about one-fifth of the drawing area).

Draw two yellow ovals to start creating the eyes.

Add black ovals to complete them.

Draw a dark gray oval to start creating the mouth.

Select the silver color you used for the robot.

Draw another silver oval over the dark oval to create a smile.

Add some lights, arms, and any other details you want.

STEP 5 – Add the Pen Extension

Click the **Code** tab, then add some extra code blocks to use the pen and drawing blocks.

 Click the **Add Extension** button.

Click **Pen**.

STEP 6 – Robot code

Drag this code into the **Scripts Area** to make the robot move around. See page 23 for help on how to choose colors.

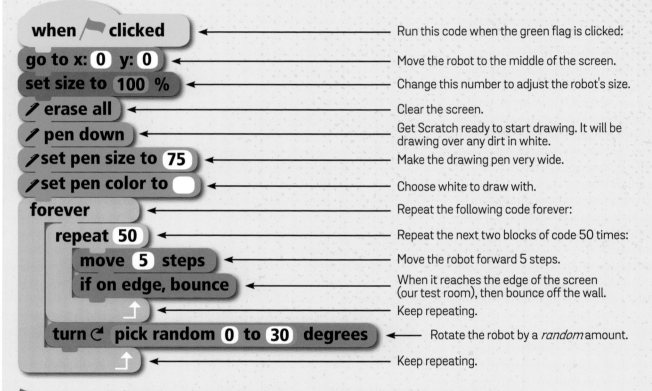

when 🚩 clicked ← Run this code when the green flag is clicked:

go to x: **0** y: **0** ← Move the robot to the middle of the screen.

set size to **100** % ← Change this number to adjust the robot's size.

✏ erase all ← Clear the screen.

✏ pen down ← Get Scratch ready to start drawing. It will be drawing over any dirt in white.

✏ set pen size to **75** ← Make the drawing pen very wide.

✏ set pen color to ⬜ ← Choose white to draw with.

forever ← Repeat the following code forever:

　repeat **50** ← Repeat the next two blocks of code 50 times:

　　move **5** steps ← Move the robot forward 5 steps.

　　if on edge, bounce ← When it reaches the edge of the screen (our test room), then bounce off the wall.

　　↑ ← Keep repeating.

　turn ↻ pick random **0** to **30** degrees ← Rotate the robot by a *random* amount.

　↑ ← Keep repeating.

 Click the flag to test your code. Your robot should start moving around the screen.

To test our robot, we need some dirt on the screen for it to clean up.

Let's draw some small dots on the screen that the robot can draw over in white.

STEP 7 – Muddy shoes

 Add some muddy shoes by clicking the **Choose a Sprite** button.

 Click **Shoes2**.

Shoes2

STEP 8 – Add the mud

 Click the **Code** tab, then add this code to make the dirt appear when you click on the screen.

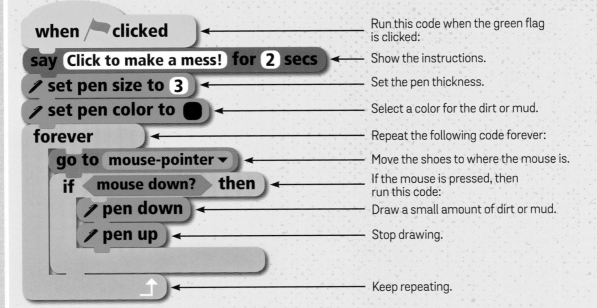

Run this code when the green flag is clicked:

Show the instructions.

Set the pen thickness.

Select a color for the dirt or mud.

Repeat the following code forever:

Move the shoes to where the mouse is.

If the mouse is pressed, then run this code:

Draw a small amount of dirt or mud.

Stop drawing.

Keep repeating.

🚩 **Click the green flag to test your code. Move the mouse around and click to make a mess! See how long it takes the robot to vacuum everything up.**

Our robot works, but it doesn't use any intelligence. It just moves around randomly.

If only there was a way we could make the robot detect where the dirt is, it would work much more effectively!

STEP 9 – Upgrade the robot

We need to add a "sensor beam" that will look for any dirt or mud.

In the **Sprites pane** click on **Sprite1**— your robot.

Click the **Costumes** tab.

STEP 10 – Add a sensor

Select the **Rectangle** tool.

Choose orange.

Drag out a long rectangle from the front of the robot to make a sensor beam. Make sure it reaches the edge of the screen.

STEP 11 – Add the Music Extension

Click the **Code** tab.

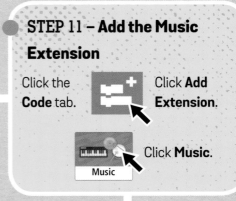

Click **Add Extension**.

Click **Music**.

Music

STEP 12 – Upgrade the code

Change your code as below.

when ⚑ **clicked**	Run this code when the green flag is clicked:
go to x: 0 **y:** 0	Move the robot to the middle of the screen.
set size to 100 %	Change this number to adjust the robot's size.
✏ **erase all**	Clear the screen.
✏ **pen down**	Get Scratch ready to start drawing.
✏ **set pen size to** 120	Make the drawing pen very wide.
✏ **set pen color to** ⬜	Choose white to draw with.
♫ **set instrument to** (21) Synth Pad ▾	Select the Synth Pad sound channel.
forever	Repeat the following code forever:
repeat until touching color ■ ?	Repeat the code below until it detects dirt:
turn ↻ 5 **degrees**	Rotate right to look somewhere else.
⤴	Keep repeating.
♫ **play note** 36 **for** 0.25 **beats**	Play a sound effect to show dirt has been found!
repeat until not touching color ■ ?	Repeat until no dirt can be found.
move 3 **steps**	Move forward slowly.
⤴	Keep repeating.
♫ **play note** 60 **for** 0.25 **beats**	Play a sound effect to show that dirt is gone.
repeat 10	Repeat this code 10 times:
move -3 **steps**	Move back slowly.
⤴	Keep repeating.
turn ↺ **pick random** 0 **to** 15 **degrees**	Rotate left a random amount.
⤴	Keep looping.

Set the color by clicking inside the square. Next, click on the pipette and then click on a color somewhere on the Stage.

touching color ⬛ ?

Create this part of the code by dropping a "not" block inside the "repeat until" block. Next, drop in a "touching color?" block.

touching color ⬛ ?

not

Investigate

What happens if you change the pen size in the robot's code from 120 to a smaller number?

Increase the amount the robot turns when it's looking for dirt. Does it still find it? If you drop dirt in the corner of the screen can the robot still find it?

Code challenge

Make your robot bigger. Does that help?

Try to adapt your code so the robot finds dirt quicker.

Create a workforce of mini robots:
- Start by changing the set size code to shrink the robot.
- Change the color of its eyes so they are not the same color as the dirt. Another robot may think they are dirt and try and vacuum them up!
- Use a "go to random position" code block at the start to prevent all the robots from starting at the same place.
- Now duplicate your mini robot a few times!

Burglar Alarm

There are many ways that technology can be used to keep us safe.

Modern buildings include smoke alarms to detect fires. Security systems can be built to check if windows or doors are opened, or to sense anyone moving around. In this project, we will make a simple alarm that will detect if anything is nearby.

STEP 1 – Get moving

Drag in these separate sections of code to make the cat move.

Run this code when the left arrow key is pressed:

Run this code when the right arrow key is pressed:

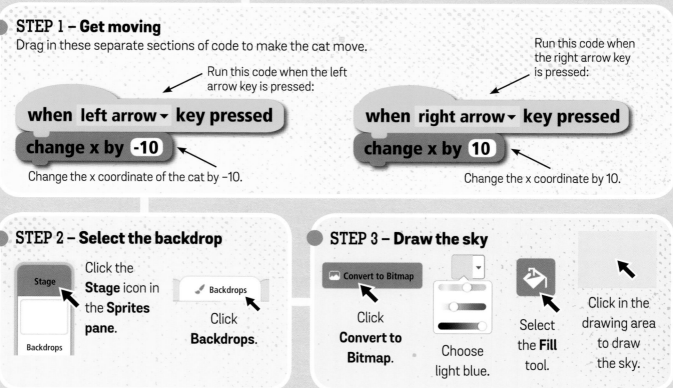

```
when left arrow ▾ key pressed
change x by -10
```

Change the x coordinate of the cat by –10.

```
when right arrow ▾ key pressed
change x by 10
```

Change the x coordinate by 10.

STEP 2 – Select the backdrop

Click the **Stage** icon in the **Sprites pane**.

Stage
Backdrops

Backdrops

Click **Backdrops**.

STEP 3 – Draw the sky

🖼 Convert to Bitmap

Click **Convert to Bitmap**.

Choose light blue.

Select the **Fill** tool.

Click in the drawing area to draw the sky.

STEP 4 – Draw the ground

Select the **Rectangle** tool, then choose green.

Set the rectangle to **Filled**.

Filled Outlined

Drag the mouse to draw the ground.

STEP 5 – The house

Draw a simple house.

See step 5 on page 7 for help.

Click the Undo tool if you make a mistake.

You can add more detail to your house when your code is finished.

STEP 6 – Add the alarm

Add an **alarm sprite** by clicking the **Choose a Sprite** icon.

Button1

Click **Button1**.

Drag the alarm onto the house.

STEP 7 – Add the Music Extension

Click **Add Extension**.

Music

Click **Music**.

STEP 8 – The code

Add the code below to make a siren sound when a noise is detected.

```
when 🏳 clicked
forever
  if  distance to sprite1 ▾  < 160  then
    ♪♪ play note 60 for 0.5 beats
  ↰
```

Run this code when the green flag is clicked:

Loop the following code forever:

If the cat is near the alarm, then run this code:

Play a sound as the alarm.

Keep looping.

🏳 **Click the flag to test your code.**

Investigate

What happens if you change the distance in the green block to a number larger than 160? How about smaller numbers?

Where is the best place to put the alarm?

Burglar Alarm (Audio)

Let's make a real burglar alarm using Scratch!

In this project, we will make a real alarm that will listen out for anyone coming near your computer! First, we need some code that can detect sound. If a sound is detected, we can make our code trigger an alarm. Your computer needs to have a built-in microphone, or you will need to plug one into it. If it has a webcam, it will probably work for sound too.

STEP 1 – **Basic code**
Drag in the code below to make a basic alarm.

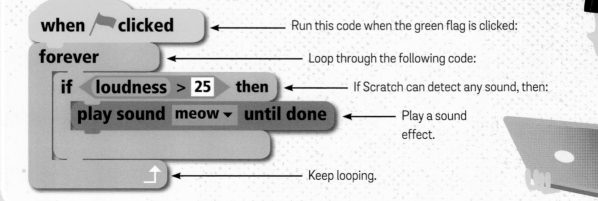

when 🚩 clicked ← Run this code when the green flag is clicked:

forever ← Loop through the following code:

if loudness > 25 then ← If Scratch can detect any sound, then:

play sound meow ▾ until done ← Play a sound effect.

← Keep looping.

STEP 2 – Test it

🚩 **Click the green flag to test your code.**

Try making a noise and see if the cat starts to meow!

> If nothing happens, check that the microphone is plugged in, then check your settings (see page 14). You may need to try a different value than 25, depending on your computer and microphone.

STEP 3 – Add the Music Extension

 Click **Add Extension.**

 Click **Music.**

STEP 4 – Alarm upgrade

Our code can detect sounds, but a cat meowing isn't going to scare off many burglars! Change your code to create a siren sound. Start by making a variable to store the *pitch* of the siren.

 Click the **Variables** category.

Click **Make a Variable.**

 Type **pitch.** Click **OK.**

STEP 5 – The siren

Change your code to include a siren by varying the pitch.

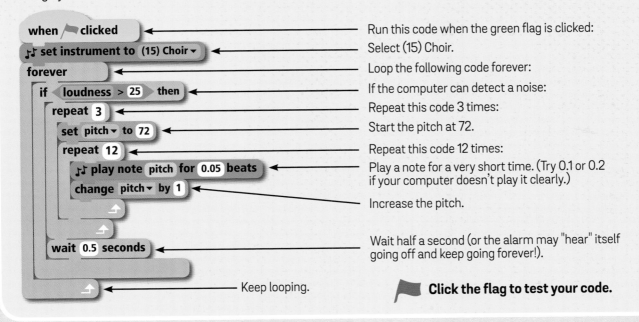

Run this code when the green flag is clicked:

Select (15) Choir.

Loop the following code forever:

If the computer can detect a noise:

Repeat this code 3 times:

Start the pitch at 72.

Repeat this code 12 times:

Play a note for a very short time. (Try 0.1 or 0.2 if your computer doesn't play it clearly.)

Increase the pitch.

Wait half a second (or the alarm may "hear" itself going off and keep going forever!).

Keep looping.

🚩 **Click the flag to test your code.**

Burglar Alarm (Video)

The previous alarm project used a microphone to detect sounds. Most burglar alarms use sensors and cameras to check for intruders.

In this next project, we'll find out how we can use the computer's webcam to detect movement and trigger an alarm sound.

STEP 1 – Make a variable

We need another variable to store the pitch of the alarm sound.

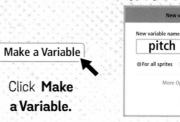

Click the **Variables** category.

Click **Make a Variable**.

Type **pitch**.

Click **OK**.

To let Scratch use your webcam you need to click the "Allow" button the first time the program runs.

Beware of other websites asking to use your webcam. Always ask an adult you trust first.

Allow

STEP 2 – Add the Music Extension

Click **Add Extension**.

Music

Click **Music**.

STEP 3 – Add the Video Extension

Click **Add Extension.**

Click **Video Sensing.**

Video sensing

STEP 4 – The code

Change your code to include a siren by varying the pitch.

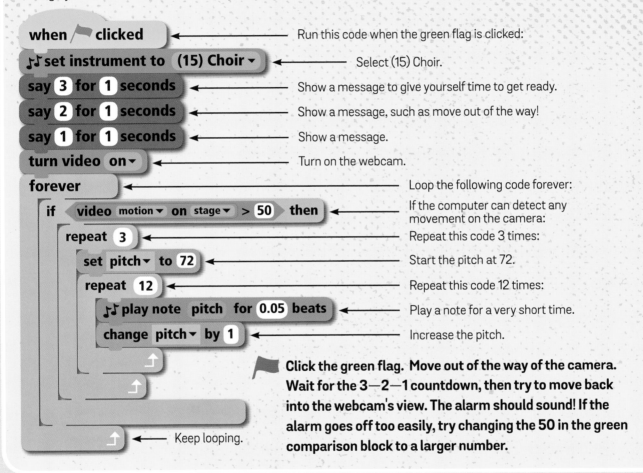

when ⚑ **clicked**	Run this code when the green flag is clicked:
♪ **set instrument to (15) Choir ▾**	Select (15) Choir.
say 3 for 1 seconds	Show a message to give yourself time to get ready.
say 2 for 1 seconds	Show a message, such as move out of the way!
say 1 for 1 seconds	Show a message.
turn video on ▾	Turn on the webcam.
forever	Loop the following code forever:
if ⟨ **video motion ▾ on stage ▾ > 50** ⟩ **then**	If the computer can detect any movement on the camera:
repeat 3	Repeat this code 3 times:
set pitch ▾ to 72	Start the pitch at 72.
repeat 12	Repeat this code 12 times:
♪ **play note pitch for 0.05 beats**	Play a note for a very short time.
change pitch ▾ by 1	Increase the pitch.
↰	Keep looping.

⚑ **Click the green flag. Move out of the way of the camera. Wait for the 3—2—1 countdown, then try to move back into the webcam's view. The alarm should sound! If the alarm goes off too easily, try changing the 50 in the green comparison block to a larger number.**

How it works

The webcam takes pictures and turns them into information that the computer can store. It does this by storing the picture as millions of tiny squares called *pixels*. The color of each pixel is stored as a number.

The video motion code block takes one photo, then it takes another photo a fraction of a second later. It compares the color stored for each pixel and checks to see how much it has changed. It then counts up the changes and uses the total to say how much motion it can detect.

Bugs and Debugging

When you find your code isn't working as expected, stop and look through each command you have put in. Think about what you want it to do, and what it is really telling the computer to do. If you are entering one of the projects in this book, check that you have not missed a line. Some things to check:

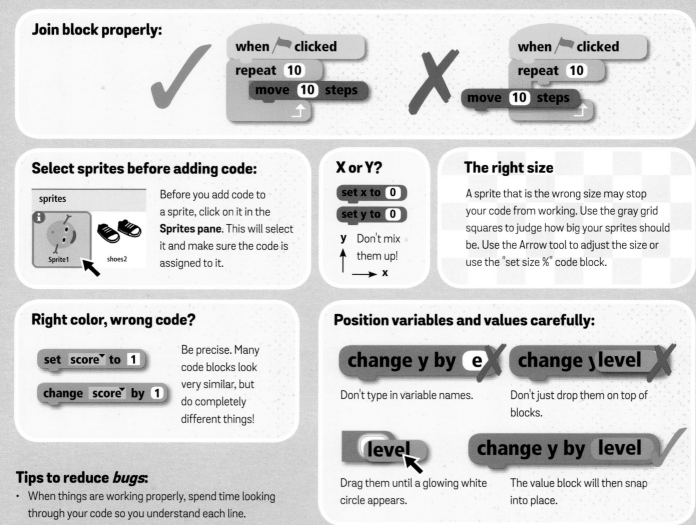

Join block properly:

when ▶ clicked
repeat 10
move 10 steps ✓

when ▶ clicked
repeat 10
move 10 steps ✗

Select sprites before adding code:

sprites
Sprite1   shoes2

Before you add code to a sprite, click on it in the **Sprites pane**. This will select it and make sure the code is assigned to it.

X or Y?

set x to 0
set y to 0

y   Don't mix
    them up!
→ x

The right size

A sprite that is the wrong size may stop your code from working. Use the gray grid squares to judge how big your sprites should be. Use the Arrow tool to adjust the size or use the "set size %" code block.

Right color, wrong code?

set score to 1

change score by 1

Be precise. Many code blocks look very similar, but do completely different things!

Position variables and values carefully:

change y by e ✗

Don't type in variable names.

change y level ✗

Don't just drop them on top of blocks.

level

Drag them until a glowing white circle appears.

change y by level ✓

The value block will then snap into place.

Tips to reduce *bugs*:

- When things are working properly, spend time looking through your code so you understand each line.

Experiment and change your code. Try out different values.

To be good at *debugging*, you need to understand what each code block does and how your code works.

- Practice debugging! Make a very short program and get a friend to change one block only, while you aren't looking. Can you fix it?
- If you are making your own program, spend time drawing a diagram and planning it before you start. Try changing values if things don't work, and don't be afraid to start again—you will learn from it.

Glossary

algorithm — Rules or steps followed to make something work or complete a task

artificial intelligence (AI) — Software that does more than just follow steps. AI systems respond with apparent intelligence to outside events.

bug — An error in a program that stops it from working properly

code block — A draggable instruction icon used in Scratch

debug — To remove bugs (or errors) from a program

degrees — The units used to measure angles

icon — A small, clickable image on a computer

loop — Repeating one or more commands a number of times

pitch — The degree of highness or lowness of a sound

pixel — A tiny square on a computer screen, combined in their thousands to display pictures

random — Not having a determined path, plan, or purpose

right-click — To click the right mouse button

sensor — A device that measures something in the real world, such as how far away an object is, and sends the answer to a computer as a number

sprite — An object with a picture on it that moves around the stage

stage — The place in Scratch where sprites move around

steps — Small movements made by sprites

system — A combination of software, hardware, sensors, and information

transparent — Something that you can see through

variable — Part of a program that stores a value that can change, for example, the score in a game

wave form — A diagram showing a sound as a wave shape where loud parts are higher, and quiet parts are lower

Index and Further Information

A
alarms, burglar 24–29

B
backdrops 5–6, 24
bugs 30

C
color, adding 7, 16–17, 19–24
command blocks 5, 8, 10–11, 13, 15, 17, 20–27, 29–30
coordinates (x, y) 8, 15, 20, 24, 30
costumes 17, 21

D
debugging 30
doorbells 12–13
drawing 5, 7, 9–11, 15–17, 19–20, 22, 24–25

E
extensions, adding 12–13, 15, 20, 22, 25, 27–29

L
lights, controlling electric 6–10, 16–17

M
microphone, using the 14–15, 17, 26–28
music, adding 12–13, 22, 25, 27, 28

P
passive infrared motion detector (PIR) 9
pixels 29

R
robots, home 18–23

S
sensors 9–10, 21–22, 28–29
sound, adding 5, 11, 15, 17, 22, 26 (*see also* music, adding)

sprite, adding a 5–6, 9, 12, 16, 18, 20–21, 24–25, 30
stage 5–6, 23, 24

V
variables 14, 27–28
video camera, adding 13, 28–29
voice controls 14–17

W
wave forms 14–15, 17
webcam, adding 13, 26, 28–29

FURTHER INFORMATION

Gifford, Clive. *Awesome Algorithms and Creative Coding.* Crabtree Publishing Company, 2015.

Wainewright, Max. *I'm a Scratch Coder.* Crabtree Publishing Company, 2018.

Woodcock, Jon. *Coding Projects in Scratch.* 2nd edition. DK Children, 2019.